BIGGEST, BADDEST BOOK OF

BEASTS

ANDERS HANSON & ELISSA MANN

Consulting Editor, Diane Craig, M.A./Reading Specialist

A Division of ABDO

ABDO
Publishing Company

visit us at www.abdopublishing.com

Published by ABDO Publishing Company, a division of ABDO, P.O. Box 398166,
Minneapolis, Minnesota 55439. Copyright © 2013 by Abdo Consulting Group, Inc.
International copyrights reserved in all countries. No part of this book may be
reproduced in any form without written permission from the publisher. Super
SandCastle™ is a trademark and logo of ABDO Publishing Company.

Printed in the United States of America, North Mankato, Minnesota
062012
092012

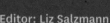
Editor: Liz Salzmann
Content Developer: Nancy Tuminelly
Cover and Interior Design and Production: Anders Hanson, Mighty Media, Inc.
Illustration Credits: Shutterstock, NOAA, Digital Vision, © Citron / CC-BY-SA-3.0
(frilled shark, p.17), Lisa Kostich (black mamba, p. 10)

Library of Congress Cataloging-in-Publication Data
Hanson, Anders, 1980-
  Biggest, baddest book of beasts / Anders Hanson and Elissa Mann.
     p. cm. -- (Biggest, baddest books for boys)
  ISBN 978-1-61783-404-2 (alk. paper)
  1. Animals--Miscellanea--Juvenile literature. I. Mann, Elissa, 1990- II. Title.
  QL49.H296 2013
  591.7--dc23
                            2011050905

Super SandCastle™ books are created by a team of professional educators, reading specialists, and
content developers around five essential components—phonemic awareness, phonics, vocabulary, text
comprehension, and fluency—to assist young readers as they develop reading skills and strategies and
increase their general knowledge. All books are written, reviewed, and leveled for guided reading, early
reading intervention, and Accelerated Reader® programs for use in shared, guided, and independent reading
and writing activities to support a balanced approach to literacy instruction.

CONTENTS

The Strange and Wonderful
Kingdom of Beasts 4

Colossal Creatures 6

Mega Mouths 8

Deadly Venom 10

The Coolest Cats 12

Big Talk for a
Little Shrimp! 14

Colorful Critters 15

Sea Dragons 16

From the Deep! 17

Don't Shoot! 18

Faces Only a Mother
Could Love 20

Platypus 22

What Do You Know About Beasts? 23

Glossary 24

THE STRANGE AND WONDERFUL
KINGDOM OF BEASTS

A beast is a wild animal. Many beasts are huge, poisonous, or scary. Some are just plain weird!

Beasts live all over the world. Some live deep in the ocean. Others live in the desert or in the forest.

FASTEST LAND ANIMAL

CHEETAH
(70 MPH,
113 KPH)

FASTEST BIRD

PEREGRINE FALCON
(200 MPH, 322 KPH)

LARGEST
CARNIVORE ON LAND

POLAR BEAR
(1,500 LB, 680 KG)

FASTEST FISH

SAILFISH (68 MPH, 110 KPH)

LARGEST ANIMAL

BLUE WHALE
(190 TONS)

COLOSSAL CREATURES

WHALE SHARK

Whale sharks are the biggest fish in the ocean! They swim with their mouths open to catch tiny animals.

AFRICAN BUSH ELEPHANT

The largest land animal is the African bush elephant. It eats 295 pounds (225 kg) of food every day. That's a lot!

KOMODO DRAGON

The Komodo dragon is the world's heaviest lizard! Some weigh more than 300 pounds (136 kg). They can smell meat from miles away.

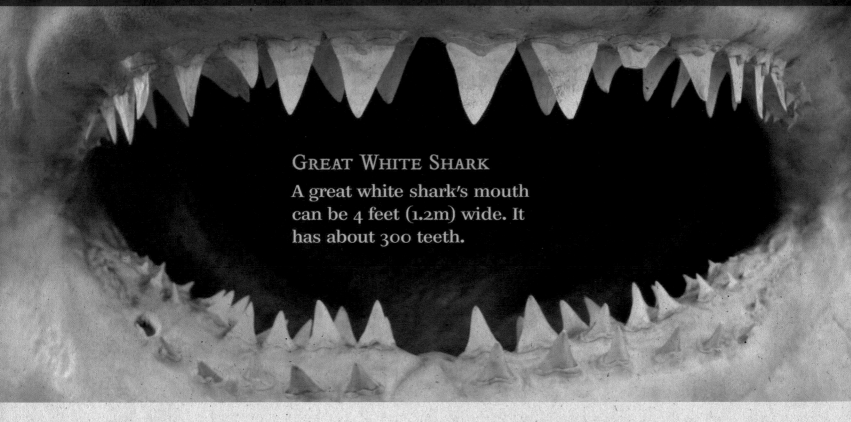

GREAT WHITE SHARK

A great white shark's mouth can be 4 feet (1.2m) wide. It has about 300 teeth.

ALLIGATOR SNAPPING TURTLE

The alligator snapping turtle is the largest freshwater turtle in North America. It lies underwater with its mouth open. When fish swim close by, the turtle grabs the fish. Snap!

HIPPOPOTAMUS

A hippo can open its mouth 4 feet (1.2 m) wide. Its **tusks** can be more than 1 foot (30 cm) long!

BABOON

Baboons are large monkeys. They have very long **canine teeth**. They show their teeth to warn enemies away.

SALTWATER CROCODILE

The saltwater crocodile is the world's largest reptile. Crocodiles have the strongest bite of any creature.

DEADLY VENOM

GILA MONSTER

SIZE: *up to 2 feet (61 cm) long*

LOCATION: *North America*

The gila monster is the only **venomous** lizard in the United States. It bites its prey hard and holds on tight. Ouch!

BLACK MAMBA

SIZE: *up to 14 feet (4 m) long*   **LOCATION:** *Africa*

The black mamba is the deadliest snake in the world. People die every year from black mamba bites. Black mambas are fast. They can slither at 12.5 miles per hour (20 kph)!

LIONFISH

SIZE: *up to 17 inches (43 cm) long*

LOCATION: *Indian Ocean, Pacific Ocean*

Lionfish look really cool! But don't get too close. This fish has a painful sting! It shoots poison out of its sharp fins.

THE COOLEST CATS

YOU KNOW ABOUT LIONS AND TIGERS. NOW LET'S MEET THEIR COOLER COUSINS!

OCELOT

Ocelots are about twice as big as house cats. They live in Central America and South America. Ocelots hunt at night.

CARACAL

Caracals live in Africa and Asia. They will attack animals up to three times their size! They are great at jumping. They can leap 10 feet (3 m).

LIGERS

Is it a tiger? Is it a lion? This cat is actually a mix of both! Ligers have a lion father and a tiger mother. Ligers only exist in zoos.

Ligers are bigger than both tigers and lions. They are the biggest cats in the world!

EURASIAN LYNX

The Eurasian lynx is the largest lynx. They live in Europe, Asia, and the Middle East. A Eurasian lynx can see a mouse 250 feet (75 m) away!

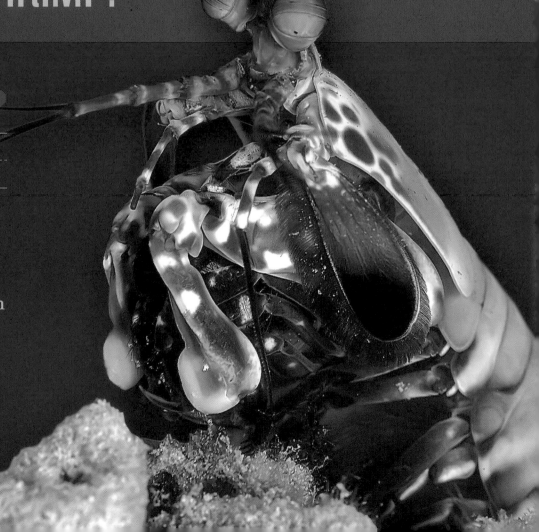

BIG TALK

FOR A LITTLE SHRIMP!

MANTIS SHRIMP

SIZE: *Up to 12 inches (30 cm) long*

LOCATION: *Indian and Pacific Oceans*

It may be small, but the mantis shrimp is very powerful.

Mantis shrimp have arms with clubs on the ends. They use them to punch their prey! The mantis shrimp's punch is the fastest movement of any animal!

COLORFUL CRITTERS

MANDRILL

The mandrill is the largest monkey. It has a red, blue, purple, and gold face. Its bottom can also have many colors, such as pink, red, blue, and purple.

CHAMELEON

Chameleons are lizards that change color! They change color for different reasons. It can be because of changes in light or temperature. They also change color when they are scared or angry.

KING VULTURE

King vultures have yellow and orange skin on their necks. Their heads can be purple, blue, or red.

SEA DRAGONS

There are two kinds of sea dragons.

Leafy sea dragons look a lot like seaweed! This helps them hide among plants in the ocean.

Weedy sea dragon

Weedy sea dragons are a little bigger than their leafy cousins. They are also more colorful.

Leafy sea dragon

FROM THE DEEP!

SCARY CRITTERS FROM THE BOTTOM OF THE SEA

DRAGONFISH

A dragonfish has a lot of sharp teeth. It also has a string-like organ growing from its chin. It's called a barbel. The barbel glows. Small fish swim toward the light. Then the dragonfish grabs them!

FRILLED SHARK

Frilled sharks live very deep in the ocean. They have needle-like teeth that are great for catching squid.

GIANT ISOPOD

The giant isopod is a **crustacean**. It lives deep in the Atlantic Ocean. Many grow to be 14 inches (36 cm) long!

DON'T SHOOT!

Don't make these creatures angry. Their built-in weapons are fully loaded!

ARCHERFISH

The archerfish shoots water out of its mouth! It aims at small bugs. It knocks the bugs into the water. Then the archerfish has a meal.

SPITTING COBRA

This snake shoots **venom** out of its **fangs**! The venom can cause blindness. The snake can hit a target more than 6 feet (2 m) away!

HORNED LIZARD

The horned lizard can shoot blood out of its eyes! This surprises its predators. And the blood tastes bad too!

VULTURE

Vultures eat rotting meat that other animals don't want. Vultures sometimes throw up on other animals to scare them away. In the summer they poop on their legs to cool off! Gross!

PROBOSCIS MONKEY

This monkey's nose can be 7 inches (18 cm) long! Their big noses make their warning calls louder.

HORSESHOE BAT

The horseshoe bat shoots sounds through its nose. Some of the sounds **bounce** off objects and head back towards the bat. By listening to those sounds, the bat knows where the objects are.

ELEPHANT SEAL

Elephant seals are the largest seals. The male elephant seal has a very large nose. It looks a little like an elephant's trunk. That's how it got its name.

PLATYPUS
THE WEIRDEST ANIMAL EVER!

At first, people thought the platypus was a joke! They thought it was too weird to be real!

There are only two **mammals** that lay eggs. The platypus is one of them!

The platypus doesn't use sight or smell to hunt. It uses its duck-like bill. The bill senses other animals in the water.

The male platypus has a **venomous** spur on each of his back legs. The platypus is the only mammal that has venom.

WHAT DO YOU KNOW ABOUT BEASTS?

1. KOMODO DRAGONS CANNOT SMELL MEAT. **TRUE OR FALSE?**

2. GREAT WHITE SHARK MOUTHS CAN BE 12 FEET WIDE. **TRUE OR FALSE?**

3. MANDRILLS ARE THE LARGEST MONKEYS. **TRUE OR FALSE?**

4. ELEPHANT SEALS HAVE LARGE NOSES. **TRUE OR FALSE?**

ANSWERS: 1) FALSE 2) FALSE 3) TRUE 4) TRUE

GLOSSARY

BOUNCE – to spring up or back after hitting something.

CANINE TOOTH – one of four pointed front teeth of a mammal.

FANG – a long, pointed tooth.

INJECT – to use something sharp to force a liquid into something.

MAMMAL – a warm-blooded animal that has hair and whose females produce milk to feed their young.

TUSK – a long, sharp tooth that sticks out of an animal's mouth.

VENOM – a poison produced by some animals that is injected into prey by biting or stinging. If something has venom, it is *venomous*.